Contents

Front cover: LHJCR 0-6-2T No 29 pilots LNER 'KI' 2-6-0 No 62005 at Moorgates, a location that epitomises the very essence of the NYMR, with the 40th anniversary train on 1 May 2013. *John Hunt*

Title page: LMS 'Black Five' 4-6-0 No 45428 *Eric Treacy* catches the low winter sun at Moorgates with a Christmas dining train on 18 December 2011. *John Hunt*

Acknowledgements

I should like to thank the photographers who have contributed pictures for this book, those who have provided advice and information, and those who have checked the content to ensure accuracy, as far as is possible! I would also like to acknowledge all the staff, volunteers, members and, of course visitors and passengers, who have made the North Yorkshire Moors Railway what it is today, because without them, and the vision of the early founders, there would be no *NYMR Recollections* as portrayed through these pages.

About the author

John Hunt has had a lifelong interest in railways, first as a trainspotter then as a photographer, which has taken him all over the world in pursuit of steam. He was an early member of the North Eastern Locomotive Preservation Group, set up in Newcastle in October 1966, and of the North Yorkshire Moors Railway. On the latter he joined the motive power department in 1970, eventually becoming a driver. A professional career in town planning was a precursor to becoming a fireman, guard, and now driver, on the main line with the West Coast Railway Company. John edits the NYMR's house magazine *Moorsline* as well as *NELPG NEWS*, and has published several railway books, including two 'Past & Present' volumes on the NYMR.

Introduction

On 5 March 1965 the railways to Whitby were decimated with the lines from Scarborough to Whitby and Rillington Junction to Grosmont closing. Only the Middlesbrough-Whitby service survived. However, local people were determined to try and save the line to Pickering, and in June 1967 the fledgling North Yorkshire Moors Preservation Society was formed. The society's aim was to restore passenger services from Grosmont to Goathland and Pickering.

The line had a fine historic pedigree, having started life as the Whitby & Pickering Railway, authorised by Act of Parliament as early as 6 May 1833, and opened throughout on 26 May 1836. It was subsequently taken over by the York & North Midland Railway in 1845, and two years later the line was extended southwards from Pickering to join the York-Scarborough line at Rillington Junction, east of Malton. Amalgamations continued, with the line coming under the auspices of the North Eastern Railway in 1854, the London & North Eastern Railway in 1923 and, finally, British Railways in 1948.

The line was the most direct route to Whitby from the south and enjoyed through coaches from and to London King's Cross, right up until the early 1960s. It also witnessed the introduction of camping coaches in 1932, providing holiday accommodation to visitors who came by train to enjoy the splendours of the North York Moors.

Sadly, together with many rural secondary lines, it was earmarked for closure under the sweeping recommendations of Dr Beeching in his famous report on the *Reshaping of British Railways* in 1963. Despite objections, closure came on 6 March 1965, when the by then diesel-worked service was augmented by a special train that ran from Scarborough to Whitby, then on to Pickering and Rillington Junction, hauled by 'K4' 2-6-0 No 3442 *The Great Marquess* and 'K1' 2-6-0 No 62005.

Following strenuous and determined efforts on the part of the preservation society and a growing legion of volunteers, the line was restored to enable some trains to occasionally traverse the whole length of the line from 1969, and from 1970 passenger trains for members were run on special occasions between Grosmont, Goathland and

Summit. Although one of the two tracks had been lifted by British Rail by the end of 1969, one line was retained, with the invaluable help of North Yorkshire County Council, so that eventually services could resume over the whole length of the line to Pickering. A big milestone was therefore reached on 1 May 1973 when the 18-mile line from Grosmont to Pickering was formally opened by HRH The Duchess of Kent.

Initially, Pickering services terminated short of the town but, following the resolving of difficulties of access, passenger trains once more graced Pickering station from May 1975. Since then the railway has gone from strength to strength, improving and consolidating its infrastructure, acquiring rolling stock, and enhancing its facilities. In recent years the NYMR has regularly carried more than 300,000 passengers a year, has a turnover of more than £3,000,000, and employs more than 100 full and part-time staff and around 300 volunteers, making it the UK's most popular heritage railway and one of the major players in the Yorkshire tourism industry. These achievements were celebrated in some style in 2013, which marked the 40th anniversary of the reopening of the line.

LEVISHAM Volunteers are the lifeblood of the NYMR, typified by Doreen Townend and Janice Leary manning Weighbridge Teas at Levisham. *Simon Barraclough*

NYMR beginnings

Following closure, these scenes at NYMR stations presented a sorry sight to the casual observer.

Below: **GOATHLAND** This is Goathland in the summer of 1969, with railbus No W79978 – the first rolling stock to arrive in the preservation era on 9 August 1968 – visible on the right. *Philip Walton*

Right: **GROSMONT** Grosmont station is viewed from the top of the tunnel in February 1969. *John Hunt*

Below right: **LEVISHAM** Weeds grow amidst rusty rails at Levisham station in 1968. *Nigel Trotter*

Left: **PICKERING** Pickering station has an air of dereliction in 1968. *John Hunt*

Right: **MOORGATES** Shortly after its arrival from the National Coal Board at Philadelphia in County Durham, and still in its NCB black livery, LHJCR 0-6-2T No 29 brings a Goathland-Summit members' train past Moorgates in August 1970. *John Hunt*

Below: **GROSMONT** NER 'P3' 0-6-0 No 2392 pilots LHJCR 0-6-2T No 29 on the Royal Train at Grosmont on 1 May 1973. Special dispensation had been given for this train to run from Whitby, but a national rail strike on the day prevented this. Instead the train backed a short way onto the Middlesbrough-Whitby line at Grosmont before drawing into the station to pick up HRH The Duchess of Kent, who performed the reopening ceremony. *John Hunt*

Whitby

Right: **WHITBY** The exterior of Whitby station is seen on 3 August 2008. The station was designed by G. T. Andrews for the Y&NMR, construction starting in 1846. It incorporated an overall roof (removed in 1952) covering two platforms and three tracks. In 1865 two further platforms were added. Rationalisation, following the 1965 closures, reduced this to just one platform, though the rebuilding of a second platform and engine release road took place in 2014. *John Hunt*

Above: **WHITBY** LNER 'K1' 2-6-0 No 62005 stands at the buffer stops in Whitby station after arrival from Pickering on 30 March 2008. The extension of NYMR services over Network Rail tracks from Grosmont to Whitby had commenced a year earlier, on 3 April 2007. *John Hunt*

Left: **WHITBY** Visiting LNER 'K4' 2-6-0 No 61994 *The Great Marquess* awaits departure from Whitby on 23 October 2007. Ironically, it was these two LNER locomotives that had worked the final steam-hauled train on closure day, 6 March 1965. *John Hunt*

WHITBY The construction of a new road to avoid the bottleneck caused by the swing bridge in the town centre meant the building of a viaduct across the River Esk and the railway. From this high vantage point BR Standard 2-6-0 No 76079 is seen leaving Whitby with the 11.00 to Pickering on 31 May 2011. On the right is the marina, above which stands Whitby Abbey, and in the distance can be glimpsed the blue waters of the North Sea. *David Rodgers*

Whitby to Grosmont

Whitby to Grosmont is 6 miles, during which the railway follows the River Esk, crossing it no fewer than nine times! It passes through Ruswarp and Sleights en route as the line meanders through the rural charm of the Esk Valley. The line was once double track but was singled in 1984.

Right: **LARPOOL VIADUCT** BR Standard 4-6-0 No 75029 *The Green Knight* passes under Larpool Viaduct with a Whitby-Pickering train on 31 March 2008. The viaduct once carried the coast line from Saltburn and Staithes to Whitby West Cliff and Scarborough, which also closed on 6 March 1965; it is now part of a long-distance footpath. *John Hunt*

Below: **LARPOOL VIADUCT** SR 'S15' 4-6-0 No 825 comes under Larpool Viaduct and hugs the bank of the River Esk with the 14.30 Whitby-Pickering train on 20 April 2009. *John Hunt*

Below right: **RUSWARP** No 825 is seen again crossing the River Esk at Ruswarp on 8 October 2009. *Maurice Burns*

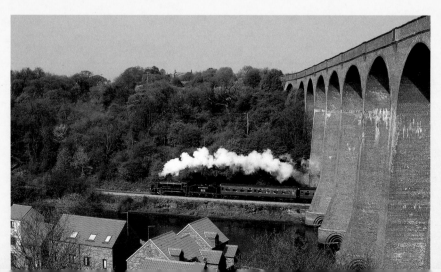

SLEIGHTS LMS 'Black Five' 4-6-0 No 45428 *Eric Treacy* accelerates away from Sleights with a Whitby-Pickering train on 1 May 2011. *Derek Phillips*

Grosmont

Grosmont is the junction with the line to Middlesbrough and was once an important industrial site with iron and brick works; remains of the latter can be glimpsed on the east side of the railway entering the station.

Right: **GROSMONT** Platforms 2, 3 and 4 are visible in this view and, strange as it may seem, in terms of the number of platforms Grosmont is the third largest station in North Yorkshire! In this view on 1 May 2013, LNER 'K1' 2-6-0 No 62005 has just arrived with the 40th anniversary special from Whitby, with LHJCR 0-6-2T No 29 ready to couple on to the front of the train to continue to Pickering, while LNER 'B1' 4-6-0 No 61264 waits to take out a service train to Pickering. *John Hunt*

Right: **GROSMONT** A flagship locomotive based on the NYMR is LNER 'A4' 'Pacific' No 60007 *Sir Nigel Gresley*, seen posing in the sunshine in Platform 2 on 26 June 2008. The 'A4' is a sister locomotive to *Mallard*, holder of the world speed record for a steam locomotive of 126mph. *John Hunt*

Above: **GROSMONT** All important stations should have a clock and Grosmont is no exception. This example originated from Northallerton and was installed in 1988. *John Hunt*

Right: **GROSMONT** The southbound exit from the station is controlled by an impressive array of semaphore signals, being passed here by LMS 'Black Five' 4-6-0 No 45407 with an arrival from Pickering on 30 April 2009. On the left LNER 'Q6' 0-8-0 No 63395 waits its next turn of duty. *John Hunt*

Above: **GROSMONT** The signals and the adjacent level crossing are controlled by the imposing signal box. The original box was located at the north end of the station in the junction of the Pickering and Middlesbrough lines, but was removed in 1980 and is now on the South Tynedale Railway in Northumberland. The present box was built to an NER design using some materials from Whitby Town signal box, has a 52-lever frame and was commissioned in 1996. Inside the box *(right)*, signaller Alistair Dalgleish is seen at work, traditional cloth in hand, on 10 March 2009. *John Hunt*

Far right: **GROSMONT** The very active Station Group designed, built and maintains this superb floral 'running-in' feature between the station and the tunnel. *John Hunt*

Grosmont to Goathland

The motive power depot is situated immediately to the south of the 1845-built, 120-yard-long Grosmont Tunnel. Beyond the MPD, the old 1836 line, now the Rail Trail, can be seen diverging to the right and today forms a very pleasant walk up to Goathland via Beckhole. Today's railway, on the 1865 deviation, and until 1969 double track, climbs at a steep 1 in 49 for the 3 miles up to Goathland, along the valley of the Murk Esk then, from Beckhole, the deep valley of the Eller Beck, both tributaries of the Esk itself. This stretch of the NYMR is a favourite place to watch and hear the locomotives working hard.

Right: **DEVIATION** LNER 'Pacific' No 60019 *Bittern* makes a rousing sight with a matching rake of 'blood and custard' coaches at Esk Valley on 4 May 2010. *Roger McDermaid*

Below: **LEASE RIGG** A public footpath runs over the tunnel to Lease Rigg. From here there is a view down into the valley, where cattle graze, oblivious to the sight and sound of SR 'S15' 4-6-0 No 825 heading a train past Esk Valley Cottages on 19 October 2011. *John Hunt*

Above: **GROSMONT** Forty years separate these two freight workhorses standing on the MPD on 4 May 2011; LNER 'Q6' 0-8-0 No 63395 was built in 1918, while BR 9F 2-10-0 No 92214 dates from 1959. Behind them are the fabrication shop, running shed, coaling plant, wheel drop and, on the right, NELPG's Deviation shed. *John Hunt*

Above left: **ESK VALLEY** A line for all seasons: viewed from Lease Rigg, LNER 'Q6' 0-8-0 No 63395 heads up the 1 in 49 on 20 April 2009. On the right lie Esk Valley Cottages, while the trackbed of the 1836 line, now a Rail Trail from Grosmont to Goathland, can be seen running just above the near fence line. *John Hunt*

Left: **ESK VALLEY** The same view on 11 February 2012 sees LNER 'J72' 0-6-0T No 69023 taking its two-coach train through the snow from Grosmont to Goathland. *John Hunt*

Above: **GREEN END** Diesels play a part on the NYMR too, at special galas, in the event of the non-availability of steam locomotives or in case of extreme fire risk. Here, during a diesel gala, 'Deltic' No D9009 *Alycidon* takes its train past Green End on 14 September 2013. *Ken Snowdon*

Top left: GREEN END The railway has a demonstration goods train that is used on special occasions. Here it is being hauled by LMS 'Black Five' 4-6-0 No 45428 *Eric Treacy* at Green End on 30 April 2011. *David Rodgers*

Bottom left: BECKHOLE Visiting the railway from the National Collection, LNWR 'G2' 0-8-0 No 49395 rounds the curve at Beckhole on 22 April 2010. *John Hunt*

Opposite: WATER ARK BRIDGE Between Beckhole and Darnholm the railway crosses the Eller Beck three times in close succession. The middle of the three crossings is Water Ark bridge, seen here with LNER 'J72' 0-6-0T No 69023 working an engineers' inspection saloon up to Goathland. The bridge is unusual since it not only carries the railway over the Eller Beck, but also crosses a footbridge that also spans the beck. *Dick Manton*

Below: WATER ARK BRIDGE Water Ark bridge can be glimpsed to the rear of the brake van is this view of LHJCR 0-6-2T No 29 working a goods train up the 1 in 49 from Grosmont to Goathland on 29 September 2013. *Ken Snowdon*

Goathland

Goathland station dates from the building of the 1865 deviation and is just a short walk from the village. It achieved fame in the 1990s as 'Aidensfield' in the long-running Yorkshire TV *Heartbeat* police series, then in 2001 as a setting for the first of the 'Harry Potter' films.

Above: **GOATHLAND** The enamel running-in board at Goathland, manufactured by Garnier & Co of Ludgate Circus, London. *John Hunt*

Top right: **GOATHLAND** BR 2-6-4T No 80072, visiting from the Llangollen Railway, brings a Grosmont-Pickering train into the busy station on 1 May 2011. It was temporarily renumbered as 80116, which was one of the Standard 2-6-4Ts tanks delivered new to Whitby in 1956. *John Hunt*

Right: **GOATHLAND** Viewed from the nearby road, across the Eller Beck, in March 2009, this view shows the Station House, the lime and coal drops, with a preserved NER hopper wagon, and on the right the goods shed, now a cafe. Beyond the drops can be glimpsed the camping coach, carrying on a tradition going back to 1932. *John Hunt*

Left: **GOATHLAND** LHJCR 0-6-2T No 29 comes through the station with a short goods train on 29 September 2013. The NER footbridge was brought from Howden, on North Tyneside, and erected in 1984. *Ken Snowdon*

Below left: **GOATHLAND** Viewed from Cow Wath bridge, a popular vantage point, LNER 'K1' 2-6-0 No 62005 restarts the NYMR's prestige 'Moorlander' dining train away from the station on 9 March 2008. Cow Wath bridge is one of only seven places where public roads cross the 18-mile NYMR. *John Hunt*

Above: **GOATHLAND** On the platform, period detail includes gas lamps, enamel advertising signs, milk churns and an LNER marker post. *John Hunt*

Below: **GOATHLAND** In the up-side sidings stand coaches for volunteer accommodation, painted in LNER tourist green and cream, and one of the NER hopper wagons about to be positioned on the coal drops. *John Hunt*

Below: **GOATHLAND** Silent sentinels: guarding the approach to the station from the south is this splendid NER-style bracket signal, which stands as testimony to the skill and dedication of the railway's Signal & Telegraph Department. *John Hunt*

Goathland to Levisham

From Goathland to Levisham is 8½ miles of contrasting scenery. South of Goathland the valley of the Eller Beck opens out, with the North York Moors evident on both sides of the railway. After 2½ miles the line reaches its summit, 553 feet above sea level, marked by a traditional steel sign, similar to the one at Stainmore on the Barnard Castle to Kirkby Stephen route. Nearby, a footpath crossing marks the Lyke Wake Walk, a strenuous 40-mile long-distance trek across the Moors from Osmotherley, near Northallerton, in the west to Ravenscar, on the North Sea coast between Robin Hoods Bay and Scarborough. After crossing Fen Bog, the line then descends at gradients as steep as 1 in 49 through Northdale and Newtondale, once a glacial overflow channel, to Levisham. There is an intermediate halt at Newtondale, opened on 23 April 1981, to serve a network of footpaths, which afford the only means of public access to these remote valleys.

Below left: **GOATHLAND** Passing the bracket signal on a snowy 7 December 2008 is SR 'S15' 4-6-0 No 825 with a Christmas dining train from Grosmont to Pickering. *Philip Benham*

Above: **GOATHLAND** The Pullman dining train again, this time headed by BR 2-6-0 No 76079, south of Goathland on 8 November 2009, with Goathland House in the background and the Eller Beck meandering in the foreground. *John Hunt*

Below: **ABBOT'S HOUSE** LMS 'Black Five' 4-6-0 No 45428 *Eric Treacy* passes Abbot's House on 1 June 2013 with a train for Pickering. Alongside the third carriage stands Goathland's down outer home signal. *John Hunt*

Above: **MOORGATES** SR 'Schools' Class 4-4-0 No 30926 *Repton* hurries a southbound dining train past Moorgates on 15 November 2009. *John Hunt*

Below: **MOORGATES** In a scene that encapsulates both the history and the scenery of the NYMR, 'S15' No 825 passes Moorgates on 23 November 2008 with another pre-Christmas dining train. In the foreground is a bridge on the original 1836 alignment, while in the background lie the moors from which the railway takes its name. *John Hunt*

Right: **MOORGATES** At the same location, this time in autumn, LNER 'Q6' 0-8-0 No 63395 heads a southbound goods train on 15 November 2007; to the right stands Sadler House and to the left Moorgates Cottages, built by the Y&NMR on the 1836 line. *John Hunt*

Below: **MOORGATES** Once again this is the same place, but from a somewhat different perspective. This time No 63395 is on a passenger train, reflected and silhouetted as the sun sinks behind Moorgates Cottages. *John Hunt*

Above: **MOORGATES** SR 'S15' 4-6-0 No 825 makes light work of
the seven-coach 'Moorlander' dining train at Moorgates on 28 October
2011. *Ken Snowdon*

Below: **ELLER BECK** BR Standard 4-6-0 No 75029 *The Green Knight*
rounds one of the curves at Eller Beck, just short of the summit of the
line, with a Grosmont-Pickering train on 5 April 2013. *John Hunt*

Above: **FEN BOG** LNER 'V2' 2-6-2 No 4771 *Green Arrow* takes the NYMR's
immaculate teak train into Northdale on 29 March 2008. To the right of the train is
Fen Bog, a waterlogged nature reserve, but a problem for the early railway builders.
In the left distance is the main Pickering-Whitby road. *Dick Manton*

Right: **NORTHDALE** From the summit at Fen Bog, the railway follows a glacial overflow channel to Pickering, seen to very good effect in this view from the edge of the moor above the ruins of Carter's House. BR Class 25 diesel No D7628 heads the lightweight 13.00 train from Pickering to Grosmont on 20 April 2013. *David Warren*

Below: **NORTHDALE** Other than by train, only parts of Northdale and Newtondale are accessible, and then only on foot. Views such as this are therefore rather rare. LNER 'Q6' 0-8-0 No 63395 brings a short goods train from Levisham to Goathland on 7 November 2011. *John Hunt*

Below right: **NEWTONDALE** Similarly, this panoramic view of Newtondale in autumn can only be enjoyed by those prepared to walk across the moors. LNER 'B1' 4-6-0 No 61264 heads up the valley with a Pickering-Grosmont train on 14 November 2013. *John Hunt*

Levisham

The village that Levisham station purports to serve lies 1½ miles away and 360 feet higher than the railway! It was therefore never conveniently located, but it controlled the end of the double track from Grosmont, after one of the tracks onwards to New Bridge at Pickering was lifted for the war effort in December 1916. After the lifting of the remaining double track in 1969, a passing loop was commissioned here in 1975 and subsequently lengthened to accommodate bigger trains. Levisham station, with its grassy paddock, is the venue for many outdoor activities, especially in the summer.

Left: **LEVISHAM** As at Goathland, there is an NER enamel running-in board at Levisham, here complete with gas lamp. *John Hunt*

Below left: **LEVISHAM** LNER 'V2' 2-6-2 No 4771 *Green Arrow* leaves Levisham northbound with the Gresley teak train on 14 March 2008. *John Hunt*

Below: **LEVISHAM** This is the station looking south on 24 April 2008. The signal box on the left has been superbly restored to working order (compare this with the picture on page 4). The station house is on the right. *John Hunt*

Right: **LEVISHAM** As at Goathland, trains regularly pass at Levisham. Here BR 2-6-0 No 76079 waits with its northbound train as SR 'West Country' 'Pacific' No 34028 *Eddystone* arrives with a train from Grosmont. *John Hunt*

Far right top: **LEVISHAM** Amidst a splendid array of autumn colours, LMS 'Black Five' 4-6-0 No 45212 departs with the dining train for Pickering on 1 November 2008. *John Hunt*

Right: **LEVISHAM** At the same location, but from the opposite side of the line, and in fitting weather conditions, the 'Black Five' leaves with a 'Santa Special' returning to Pickering on 7 December 2008. *Philip Benham*

Far right bottom: **LEVISHAM** A driver's-eye view from LMS 'Black Five' 4-6-0 No 44871 as it prepares to pass sister locomotive No 45428 *Eric Treacy* at Levisham on 7 April 2011. *John Hunt*

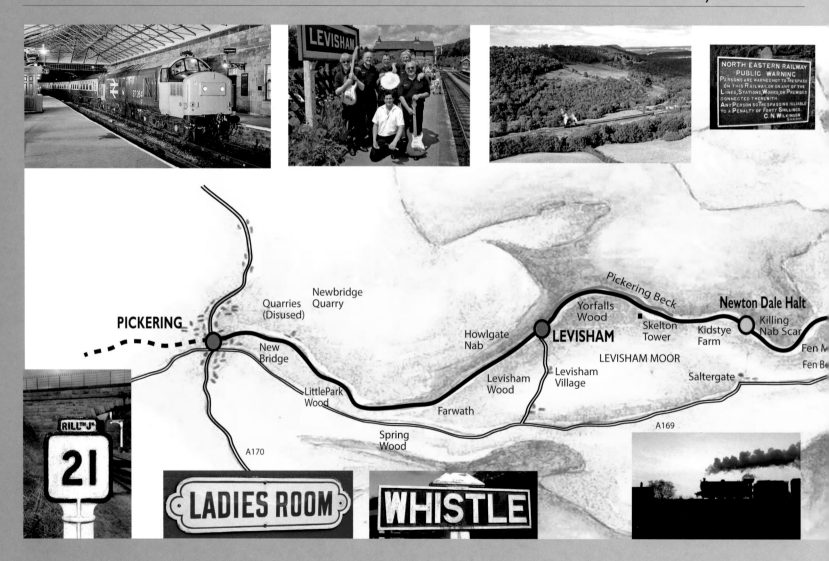

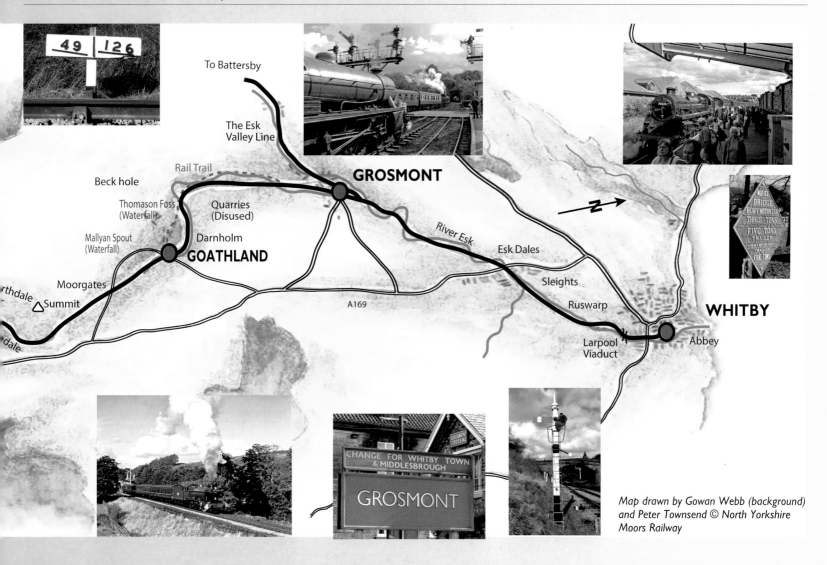

To Battersby

The Esk
Valley Line

Rail Trail

Beck hole

GROSMONT

Thomason Foss
(Waterfall)

Quarries
(Disused)

Mallyan Spout
(Waterfall)

Darnholm

GOATHLAND

River Esk

Esk Dales

Moorgates

Sleights

rthdale
△ Summit

A169

Ruswarp

WHITBY

dale

Larpool
Viaduct

Abbey

*Map drawn by Gowan Webb (background)
and Peter Townsend © North Yorkshire
Moors Railway*

Levisham to Pickering

The 6-mile section from Levisham to Pickering is mostly inaccessible until the outskirts of Pickering at New Bridge. It includes the longest stretch of straight track on the whole railway, nearly 1¾ miles, more than a mile of which was completely relaid in 2014. From Farwath to Kingthorpe the line passes through woodlands of the Duchy of Lancaster and, approaching New Bridge, on the left-hand side, recent extensive works designed to alleviate flooding in Pickering.

Right: **FARWATH** LMS 'Black Five' 4-6-0 No 45428 *Eric Treacy* heads past Farwath with a train from Pickering to Grosmont in October 1998. *John Hunt*

Below: **FARWATH** LMS 'Crab' 2-6-0 No 42765 takes a goods train, bound for Pickering, past Farwath in October 1997. *John Hunt*

Below right: **KINGTHORPE CURVE** LMS 'Black Five' 4-6-0 No 45407 accelerates round Kingthorpe curve with a Grosmont-Pickering train in October 2003. *John Hunt*

Above : **NEW BRIDGE** LMS 'Black Five' 4-6-0 No 45212 pulls away from New Bridge at Park Gate with a Pickering-Grosmont train on 20 October 2010. *John Hunt*

Above: **NEW BRIDGE** No 45212 is seen again, this time on a 'Santa Special', leaving New Bridge on 21 December 2010. *John Hunt*

Pickering

Pickering, a market town of medieval origin with a castle dating back to the late 11th century, has a population of around 6,300. It is the administrative headquarters of the NYMR and the southern terminus of the line, which once continued south towards Rillington Junction, but this was closed in 1966 and lifted by 1970. Over recent years the station has benefited from extensive refurbishment and extensions, including a visitor centre, learning centre, the NYMR archives, footbridge, demonstration signal box, shop, cafe, ticket office, toilets and customer services, not to mention reinstatement, after 60 years, of the overall roof.

Above: **PICKERING** LNER 'V2' 2-6-2 No 60800 *Green Arrow* leaves Pickering past a traditional LNER running-in sign, made out of whitewashed bricks and edging, in May 2005. *John Hunt*

Left: **PICKERING** Just north of the station lies the railway's only turntable, which came from York North MPD, later the National Railway Museum, and was installed in the original pit in 1993; it is seen here with BR Standard 4-6-0 No 75014 being turned in January 1996. *John Hunt*

Above: **PICKERING** The footbridge came from Walkergate, Newcastle, and was re-erected in 1996. In this view from the bridge BR 2-6-4T No 80072 attracts admiring glances as it enters the station from Grosmont on 11 May 2012. *John Hunt*

Above right: **PICKERING** With hoar frost on the trees and welcoming Christmas lights, BR 2-6-4T No 80135 brings a 'Santa Special' from Levisham into the station on 22 December 2006. *Philip Benham*

Right: **PICKERING** With some feathered friends to greet it, LNER 'A4' 'Pacific' No 4464 *Bittern*, on a matching set of teak coaches, enters the station under the impressive new overall roof on 4 May 2012. *John Hunt*

Above: **PICKERING** Like Grosmont, Pickering has its station clock. Below it is a replica NER tiled map, identical to those still to be found at stations such as Whitby, York, Middlesbrough and Scarborough. *John Hunt*

Above: **PICKERING** Part of the NER map showing the present NYMR and associated lines. *John Hunt*

Far right top: **PICKERING** As at all the NYMR stations, the floral displays, so carefully tended by the respective Station Groups, add seasonal colour for the enjoyment of visitors. *John Hunt*

Right: **PICKERING** As part of the 'Trains of Thought' project, a visitor and interpretation centre has been provided on Platform 2 in the old 19th-century pump house. *John Hunt*

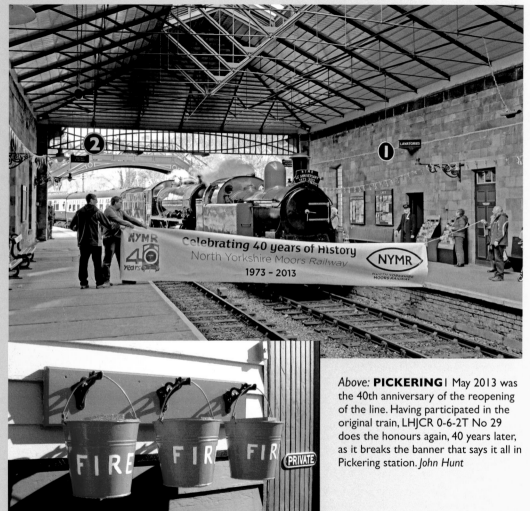

Above: **PICKERING** On the west side of the station, behind Platform 2, is a picnic area protected by a section of the station canopy recovered from Church Fenton. This is just part of the development of the station under the award-winning 'Train of Thought' umbrella. *John Hunt*

Right: **PICKERING** The station sports the LNER green and cream paint scheme, shown to good effect here, with traditional fire buckets. *John Hunt*

Above: **PICKERING** 1 May 2013 was the 40th anniversary of the reopening of the line. Having participated in the original train, LHJCR 0-6-2T No 29 does the honours again, 40 years later, as it breaks the banner that says it all in Pickering station. *John Hunt*

Shops and catering

Above: **GROSMONT** The NYMR's immaculate Pullman dining train stands in Platform 3 at Grosmont; nearest the camera is Pullman Brake 3rd No 79, built by Metropolitan Carriage in 1928. *John Hunt*

Top right: **PULLMAN CAR No 79** These diners are clearly enjoying themselves in the opulent surroundings of Pullman Car No 79. *John Hunt*

Right: **PULLMAN CAR** *OPAL* Diners being served inside Pullman car *Opal*, a Metro-Cammell 1st Parlour Car built in 1960. *John Hunt*

Above left and above: **GOATHLAND** The award-winning cafe at Goathland was tastefully converted from the old goods shed in 2000; it retains the loading crane and wooden entrance doors, and customers are seated in two former Hull & Barnsley Railway wagons. *John Hunt*

Left: **PICKERING** Pickering station was extensively refurbished in 1999/2000, when a purpose-built shop was created, seen here. *John Hunt*

Special events

Above: **LEVISHAM** The paddock at Levisham plays host to frequent special events, including traditional Punch and Judy shows, seen here, real ale festivals, live music, wartime weekend activities (when it becomes the mythical French town of Le Visham), and vintage vehicles. *John Hunt*

Below: **GROSMONT** At Grosmont, Company B perform 1940s musicals. *John Hunt*

Above: **GROSMONT** One of the longest-running special events is the visit of Santa Claus at Christmas. Here he greets young and old at Grosmont. *John Hunt*

Right: **'SOMEWHERE IN ENGLAND'** Another long-running and extremely successful traditional event is Wartime Weekend, held every October. Both the railway and Pickering town itself wind the clock back to the 1940s. Here, re-enactors representing Winston Churchill and Lord Montgomery converse 'somewhere in England'! *John Hunt*

Left: **PICKERING** A ride on the NYMR can be a unique experience, so the railway is often the venue for wedding celebrations, as Amy and Jon can no doubt testify on 20 August 2011.

Right: **GOATHLAND** Every July there is a Vintage Vehicle Weekend, when some memorable and magnificent cars, lorries, buses and motor cycles vie with the regular steam locomotives to command visitors' attention. This is a typical scene at Goathland. *Ian Wolstencroft*

Left: **LEVISHAM** At one of the 1960s music events at Levisham, Jive Express are seen in full swing. *Simon Barraclough*

Bottom left: **MOORGATES** The NYMR also hosts rather eccentric activities such as what has now become a regular out-of-season fixture, the annual Velocipede Rally! Here, human-powered, home-made velocipedes are seen at full throttle at Moorgates on 7 November 2013. *John Hunt*

Right: **WHITBY** As a prelude to the London Olympics, the Olympic torch was carried on the railway from Whitby to Pickering; it is pictured here at Whitby prior to its historic run on 18 June 2012. *John Hunt*

Above: **GROSMONT** At Grosmont the motive power depot is located just south of the tunnel. Development of the site started in 1973 and has been incrementally enlarged ever since. Here, steam and diesel locomotives are serviced, maintained and overhauled. In this scene, SR 'Schools' Class 4-4-0 No 30926 *Repton* and the frames, minus boiler, of LMS 'Black Five' 4-6-0 45428 *Eric Treacy* receive attention inside the main workshop on 25 March 2009. *John Hunt*

Left: **PICKERING** While the majority of the railway's coaches are former BR Mark 1 vehicles from the 1950s and '60s, the LNER Coach Association is responsible for acquiring and restoring the line's splendid teak train. Here No 1623, a BR-built steel-panelled 3rd Class corridor compartment coach from 1950, though to a pre-nationalisation Thompson design, has the teak-effect 'scumbling' applied by Dave Simpson of the SRPS, inside the LNERCA's Pickering workshop, opened in 2008. *Malcolm Brown*

Below: **PICKERING** The Carriage & Wagon Department's works is situated at Pickering, adjacent to the station. It includes a two-road workshop, erected in 1983, and a paint shop. Here coach No E9235, a Brake 2nd Open built at Doncaster in 1955, receives serious bodywork repairs. *Jerry Hawley*

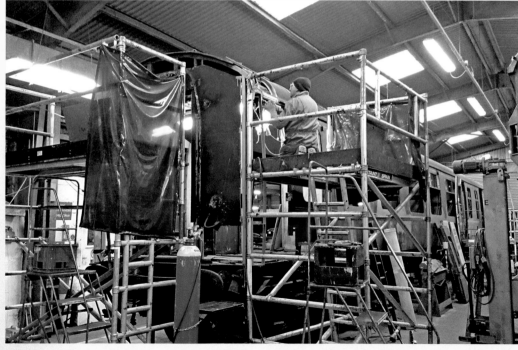

Top left: **GROSMONT** Outside the fabrication shop, the railway's Cowan Sheldon steam crane, built for the LNER in 1926 and capable of lifting 45 tons, moves a steam locomotive boiler on 2 April 2008. *John Hunt*

Bottom left: **NEW BRIDGE** The other main workshop on the NYMR is the Permanent Way Department's headquarters at New Bridge, a mile north of Pickering station. It is here that track materials are loaded and unloaded, trackwork assembled, ballast stored and PW wagons, machines and plant based, maintained and overhauled in a two-road shed built in 1993. A steam locomotive servicing facility and pit were added in 2006. *John Hunt*

Filming

Below: **MOORGATES** The NYMR, or more specifically Goathland, was the setting for part of the first 'Harry Potter' film, *Harry Potter and the Philosopher's Stone*, released in 2001. South of Goathland, the airborne camera crew follow GWR 'Hall' Class 4-6-0 No 5972 *Hogwarts Castle* (in reality *Olton Hall*) at Moorgates on a filming run into Northdale on 5 October 2000. *John Hunt*

Above left: **'HOGWARTS'** This scene at 'Hogwarts', photographed from No 5972 *Hogwarts Castle*, shows crew and cast, including Ron Weasley, taking a break from filming in October 2000. *John Hunt*

Left: **'HOGWARTS'** *Hogwarts Castle* is surrounded by film crew and extras in Goathland – or rather 'Hogwarts' - station in October 2000. *John Hunt*

Above: **BECKHOLE** Long associated with the NYMR is *Heartbeat*, the highly successful and long-running TV series featuring Goathland as 'Aidensfield'. This police drama, set in North Yorkshire, ran for 18 series between 1992 and 2010. During a break in filming, stars of the series Derek Fowlds (Sergeant Oscar Blaketon), Nick Berry (PC Nick Rowan) and Mark Jordan (PC Phil Bellamy) pose for the camera at Beckhole. *John Hunt*

Locomotíves

Right: **GROSMONT** LNER 'A1' 'Pacific' No 60163 *Tornado* and BR 2-6-0 No 76079, under the coaling plant, are prepared for their day's work at Grosmont MPD on 31 May 2011. The purpose-built coaling plant, erected in 1996, is believed to be the only one of its kind in the UK. *David Rodgers*

Below: **GROSMONT** Inside the running shed there is an LNER flavour as 'V2' 2-6-2 No 4771 *Green Arrow* keeps company with 'A4' 4-6-2 No 60007 *Sir Nigel Gresley* and 'B1' 4-6-0 No 61264 on 24 April 2008. *John Hunt*

Right: **GROSMONT** Super power! The imposing front ends of BR 8MT 4-6-2 No 71000 *Duke of Gloucester* and BR 9F 2-10-0 No 92214 *Cock o' the North* at Grosmont on 30 April 2011. *Howard Smith*

Left: **GROSMONT** A close-up of the motion of BR Standard 4-6-0 No 75029 *The Green Knight.* *John Hunt*

Right: **GROSMONT** The NYMR offers footplate experience courses, and here two participants (middle and left), together with fireman Ray Stewart, pose for the camera after emptying out the smokebox char from GWR 2-6-2T No 4277 on 8 May 2008. *John Hunt*

Left: **PICKERING** Two more LNER favourites, this time 'little and large': 'B1' 4-6-0 No 61264, masquerading as No 61002 *Impala* (the last 'B1' to work over the railway in BR days) and 'J72' 0-6-0T No 69023 stand side by side at Pickering on 7 May 2013. *John Hunt*

Carriage & Wagon

Right: **PICKERING** Fresh out of the paint shop at Pickering is coach No E4839, a BR Mark 1 Tourist 2nd Open, typical of the NYMR fleet, while beyond it stands Gresley teak BTK coach No 3669. *John Hunt*

Below: A glimpse inside one of No 3669's compartments, showing the excellent finish achieved by members of the LNERCA. *John Hunt*

Above: **GOATHLAND** The six-wheel Express Dairy milk tank wagon, No B3192, built at Derby in 1952, stands at Goathland. *Ian Broadhead*

Left: **SADLER HOUSE** The NYMR has a demonstration goods train made up of a variety of wagons typical of the BR period. It is seen here at Sadler House, south of Goathland, behind LNER 'Q6' 0-8-0 No 63395 on 16 November 2011. Above the locomotive can be seen the radar building of RAF Fylingdales. *John Hunt*

Above: **GOATHLAND** This fully restored BR 20-ton brake van, No B954854, built at Faverdale in 1959, is also seen at Goathland. The NYMR Wagon Group is responsible for the upkeep of this valuable part of the NYMR's heritage. *Ian Broadhead*

Major projects

Two major projects have put the NYMR at the forefront of the railway heritage sector. The first of these was the renewal of bridge 30, located in a spot, initially inaccessible by road, between Grosmont and Goathland. The renewal also coincided with almost continuous lying snow and sub-zero temperatures, a testing challenge to all concerned. The second project was the reinstatement of the overall roof at Pickering station, originally removed back in 1952. The pictures on these two pages show the work being carried out.

Above: **BRIDGE 30** Work took place day and night. With snow on the ground, one of the main girders is cut free, as the crane takes the weight, at 18.18 on 19 January 2010. *John Hunt*

Below: **BRIDGE 30** With the snow still lying, the new bridge is craned into place on 11 February 2010. *John Hunt*

Above: **BRIDGE 30** The formal commissioning of the new bridge was performed by impresario Pete Waterman, seen here being interviewed for TV on 19 April 2010. *John Hunt*

Below: **BRIDGE 30** With the work complete, BR 2-6-0 No 76079 brings a passenger train over the new bridge on 17 April 2010. *David Warren*

Above: **BRIDGE 30** Bridge 30 before demolition on 10 January 2009. *John Hunt*

Above: **PICKERING** The new roof, the Yorventure visitor centre, archive and Reussner learning centre were all part of the 'Train of Thought' project, which was the recipient of a National Railway Heritage Award in 2012. *John Hunt*

Above: **PICKERING** The view inside Pickering station on 25 March 2011. *John Hunt*

Left: **PICKERING** A close-up of the roof trusses and glazing designed to replicate the original G. T. Andrews design. *John Hunt*

Right: **PICKERING** The formal unveiling of the new roof was performed by HRH The Duke of Kent on 4 October 2011. *John Hunt*

Volunteering

Right: **A4 FOOTPLATE** Senior driver Gerry Skelton at the controls of an 'A4' 'Pacific'. *John Hunt*

Below: **GROSMONT** In the MPD machine shop, fitter Keith Pardy machines the little end of a steam locomotive's connecting rod. *John Hunt*

Above right: **GROSMONT** The future? A team of enthusiastic Junior Volunteers pose for the camera at Grosmont MPD on 21 August 2011. Regular organised programmes are put together several times a year to encourage younger enthusiasts, under adult supervision, to help out in all areas of the railway in the hope that they will be the staff of the future. *Roger Swift*

Right: **GROSMONT** Diesel fitters Bob Fussey and Nick Simpson remove the piston from a diesel locomotive's power unit. *John Hunt*

Far right: **GROSMONT**: Junior Volunteers clean LNER 'N2' 0-6-2T No 1744 at Grosmont. *Roger Swift*

Above: **PICKERING** What an under-repair open coach looks like with no seats or tables! A member of the C&W staff effects repairs. *John Hunt*

Above: **NEW BRIDGE** Lettering skills are put to good use by Nick Carter on No DE900572, an independent snow plough built for the NER at York in 1909. *Ian Broadhead*

Above left: **GROSMONT** In the bowels of Grosmont Crossing signal box, S&T engineer David Torbet is seen at work. *John Hunt*

Above right: **LEVISHAM** Under floodlights, the level crossing at Levisham is renewed by night on 2 February 2012. *Simon Barraclough*

Above: **PICKERING** Other volunteers, part of the NYMR's Wagon Group, carry out repairs to No B894178, a BR Swindon-built cattle wagon of 1952 vintage. *Ian Broadhead*

Above: **NEW BRIDGE** Work on the track and infrastructure is carried out at all times of the day and night, and in all weathers. Here, in almost white-out conditions, track relaying continues at New Bridge on 14 January 2013. *John Hunt*

Above: **GROSMONT** Five members of the S&T gang are busy reassembling the signal 'dolls' to be placed on the new signal gantry that came from Falsgrave, Scarborough, and is now re-erected at Grosmont. *Craig Donald*

Left: **GREEN END** Before and after... Borrows 0-4-0WT No 3, built in 1898, and at that time in the custody of the Newcastle University Railway Society, arrived at the NYMR on 28 March 1969 and was used on early works trains. It is seen here pulling a Hull & Barnsley Railway Brake 3rd coach at Green End, between Grosmont and Goathland, on 27 April 1969, the first 'passenger train' on then embryonic NYMR, and before BR had lifted the second track. No 3 is now on the Tanfield Railway awaiting restoration. *John Boyes*

Right: At the same location 38 years later, LNER 'Q6' 0-8-0 No 63395 takes a goods train up the 1 in 49 on a beautifully autumnal 16 November 2007. *John Hunt*

Index of locomotives

Glossary

GWR	Great Western Railway
SR	Southern Railway
LMS	London Midland & Scottish Railway
LNER	London & North Eastern Railway
NER	North Eastern Railway
Y&NMR	York & North Midland Railway
BR	British Railways
LHJCR	Lambton, Hetton & Joicey Colliery Railway
NCB	National Coal Board
MPD	Motive Power Department
C&W	Carriage & Wagon
S&T	Signal & Telegraph
NYMR	North Yorkshire Moors Railway